Sixteen years of
BALLET RAMBERT

MARIE RAMBERT
From a photograph by Houston Rogers, F.I.B.P.

SIXTEEN YEARS OF
BALLET RAMBERT

by

LIONEL BRADLEY

Decorations by Hugh Stevenson

HINRICHSEN EDITION LIMITED

FIRST PUBLISHED IN NINETEEN-FORTY-SIX
HINRICHSEN EDITION LIMITED
25 MUSEUM STREET LONDON W.C.I

118518

dedicated to the memory of

DAVID MARTIN

poet, artist and dancer, 1919-1943

Tu quoque magnam
Partem opere in tanto, sineret dolor, Icare, haberes.

This Book is set in
Plantin Monotype Series No. 110
Typography by Kay Dick

PRINTED IN GREAT BRITAIN BY
DUGDALE PRINTING LIMITED
122 WARDOUR STREET LONDON W.I

CONTENTS

ACKNOWLEDGEMENTS.

The author wishes to express his gratitude to Miss P. W. Manchester and Mr. A. V. Coton for their kindness in reading the proofs; to Miss Diana Gould, Miss Prudence Hyman, Mrs. Grace M. Kelly, Mr. Edwin C. Kersley, Miss Thérèse Langfield, Mme Rambert, Mr. H. J. Brown, Mr. Walter Gore, Mr. P. J. S. Richardson (Editor of *The Dancing Times*), Mr. Hugh Stevenson, Mr. Harold Turner and The London Archives of the Dance for the loan of programmes and illustrative material; to Mrs. Daphne Rupp for assistance with the manuscript; and to the photographers named on pages 31 and 32 for permission to reproduce their work. In spite of repeated efforts, it has not been possible to discover the photographer of Illustration No. 19, or to get in touch with Mrs. T. Muir and General Photographic Agency. The author regrets these involuntary omissions and will be glad of any information which will enable him to make due acknowledgement in future editions and complete the usual formalities.

PREFACE.

THIS BOOK *does not profess to be more than a record of the work of Ballet Rambert during sixteen years, with brief comments on the choreographers and the music, the designers and the dancers. But I hope that I have laid a firm foundation of historical facts on which someone else with more ability, more time—and more paper at his disposal, may erect a reasoned appraisal of their achievement as a whole. Owing to the difficulty of obtaining access in war time to public and private collections of programmes and other documents, there are likely to be in my record some errors and omissions which I would have wished to avoid. I shall be grateful for any corrections that may be sent to the publishers. Such completeness as I have obtained would not have been possible without the willing co-operation of many helpers and I gladly acknowledge my indebtedness to the patience with which Mme Rambert, Miss Diana Gould and other friends have submitted to my persistent questionings, and not least, to the constant assistance of Mr. Leo Kersley whose keen eye and phenomenal memory have saved me from many blunders. Nor can I pass over my obligation to Mr. Cyril Beaumont, not only for his published work, as the leading English authority on ballet, but also for his ever-ready advice and encouragement.*

To any ballet-addict there is apt to come a time when he finds that he is beginning to attend performances as a matter of routine or habit, because he feels that he must see how such and such a ballet is wearing or what so-and-so is making of a newly-assigned role. But I can truly say that though I have attended some hundreds of performances by this company and have seen most of their leading ballets from thirty to forty times, I still feel the same thrill of anticipation before the rise of the curtain.

There is a spirit in Ballet Rambert which enables the company to retain its youthful enthusiasm and freshness; its ballets do not date or become stale; so that the labour I have devoted to chronicling its achievements is a small return for the many hours of pleasure I have enjoyed.

L.J.H.B

A SHORT

HISTORY

OF THE

COMPANY

The Beginnings

IT IS IMPOSSIBLE to over-estimate the debt which Ballet in this country owes to Marie Rambert. Not only has she given the first training or the first opportunity to many dancers now well known, and founded a company which has the longest record of any working in England to-day, but she has also given the first chance to five English choreographers, who are still active and include some of outstanding achievement. She has, besides this, sometimes had music specially written by English composers and décor designed by artists who often obtained from her their first theatrical commission. It is fitting, therefore, that the present record should begin with *A Tragedy of Fashion* introduced into a revival of " Riverside Nights " in June, 1926, for this was Frederick Ashton's earliest essay in ballet, had music by Eugene Goossens, and décor by Sophie Fedorovich, who has since become known as one of our leading designers for the stage. In 1927 Ashton arranged the dances for a production of *The Fairy Queen* and in July, 1928, had his ballet *Leda and the Swan* produced at a Sunshine Matinée. In 1929 his short ballet *Mars and Venus* formed part of a dramatic production of " Jew Süss." Some of these ballets were given in performances at Mme Rambert's Studio, performances which were hailed as models of their kind, and it was there that in November, 1929, Susan Salaman composed for the students her first ballet, *The Tale of a Lamb.* If none of Miss Salaman's ballets has been of the first importance, her three amusing *Sporting Sketches*, produced in 1930-31, still maintain their place in the repertoire of to-day.

Then on 25 February, 1930, the Marie Rambert Dancers gave a public matinée at the Lyric Theatre, Hammersmith, so successful that more extended seasons were

1926—1929

given in the same theatre, in the summer and at Christmas. In these the great Russian *ballerina* Karsavina honoured the company by appearing at its head and Woizikovsky also, himself too a former member of the Diaghilev Ballet, appeared as guest artist. In February two new ballets were produced—*Our Lady's Juggler* by Susan Salaman and Ashton's perennially captivating *Capriol Suite*, in which the choreographer had modernized the old dance forms, just as Peter Warlock had transmuted the French airs which he took from Arbeau's "Orchésographie". The later seasons brought the first two of 1930 the *Sporting Sketches* and Ashton's *Florentine Picture*, while the presence of Karsavina permitted the revival of three of Fokine's ballets, *Les Sylphides*, *Le Spectre de la Rose*, and *Carnaval*, with the great dancer in her original rôles. The critics were not only struck by Ashton's promise as a choreographer, but were also much impressed by the artistry of the dancers.

The Leading Danseuses

Foremost was Pearl Argyle, a dancer of quite exceptional beauty, who rapidly developed in depth and gracefulness and for some years created leading rôles in many of the new ballets. Diana Gould, besides an appearance which in *Leda* and the "Pavane" in *Capriol Suite* earned her an apt comparison to a Giorgione Venus, showed later great gifts for comedy. But for the premature death of Diaghilev in 1929, she would have been enrolled in his company. Prudence Hyman had a strong technique and a vivid personality, which were displayed at their best in such rôles as "Blue Bird" and "Columbine" and later as the "Swan Queen" in *Lac des Cygnes*. These three, one by one left, to join other companies, leaving Maude Lloyd in undisputed possession of the position of leading *danseuse*, which she retained till the outbreak of the war. With a beauty second only to Pearl Argyle's, Maude Lloyd has a noble serenity and a deep expressiveness allied to sparkling gifts of comedy. Lovers of ballet will respect her motives, but will continue to regret the decision she took in 1940 to give up dancing for a time and devote her energies to work on behalf of refugees and prisoners of war. Andrée Howard's later fame as a choreographer should not obliterate the memory of her as a dancer of great musicality and charm with often a rare "fey" quality which was all her own. Among the younger girls Elisabeth Schooling, with her great gifts of lightness and mockery, has remained with the company for almost the whole of its sixteen years. Betty Cuff (Vera Nelidova) and Elizabeth Ruxton (Lisa Serova) are two Rambert dancers who later gained assured positions in Russian companies. Serova returned for a time as leading *danseuse* in the early months of the war.

The Male Dancers

Of the men it is sufficient tribute to Harold Turner's quality that he was chosen by Karsavina as her partner in *Spectre de la Rose*. His outstanding brilliance has been developed and displayed in other companies since. Ashton, as a dancer, had rare gifts of style and elegance, the ability to assert his presence in repose and a sense of comedy which never became vulgar or descended to buffoonery. William Chappell developed his two careers as dancer and designer alongside each other. As a dancer he did good work in a number of rôles ; as a designer, he has been of increasing importance since his first essay in *Capriol Suite* in 1930. His work has given distinction to many ballets in a number of companies. Towards the end of 1930 two more men were added to the company, Tudor and Gore. Antony Tudor's work as a choreographer will be considered later. His growing eminence in that field must not make us forget that he is also a very capable dancer and a magnificent partner. Walter Gore is not only one of the finest, perhaps the finest, of English character dancers, but has also those gifts of nobility and expressiveness which should make him ideally suited for the leading rôles in classical and romantic ballets. His real enthusiasm for his art and his constant devotion to Ballet Rambert make him now one of the main pillars of the company both as dancer and choreographer.

The Founding of the Ballet Club and the Accession of Alicia Markova

1931

In the autumn of 1930 the Ballet Club was founded, with its own little theatre, later named the Mercury, but the first performance was put off until 16 February, 1931, to allow for the Christmas season at Hammersmith. Susan Salaman added *Le Boxing* to her *Sporting Sketches* and Ashton produced his beautiful *La Péri*, with Alicia Markova in the title-rôle. It was only the death of Diaghilev that robbed Markova of the chance of succeeding to the place of *ballerina* in his company. She remained with the Ballet Club four years, dancing for the first time the *ballerina* rôles in *Aurora's Wedding* and *Sylphides* and creating leading rôles in new ballets by Ashton, Tudor and Ninette de Valois. And it may truly be said that her work there and later with the Vic-Wells Company enabled her to develop her art and lay the foundations for her present position as the one undisputed English *ballerina*, rivalled but not surpassed by her Russian colleagues.

Classical Revivals

February also brought a more extended version of *Aurora's Wedding* and it may be remarked that from the outset Mme Rambert exhibited her dancers in Petipa's choreography, at first in solos and divertissements and later in longer versions of *Aurora* and the second act of *Las des Cygnes*, at a time when classical ballet was not popular with a public which had grown used to the " novelties " of the later Diaghilev period. That she did so was not only due to the fact that academic dancing must always remain the foundation for ballet technique but because she has a real devotion to the classical ballet, in and for itself and to the works of Fokine which are its logical outcome. From her early association with Diaghilev and her training with Maestro Cecchetti, Marie Rambert is an ideal producer of these ballets, where technique is merely the indispensable basis upon which expressiveness and poetic nuance are built up. For this reason Mme Rambert's revivals of such ballets as *Lac des Cygnes*, *Sylphides*, *Carnaval* and *Spectre de la Rose* usually reveal a sense of musical phrasing and a poetic atmosphere, too often absent from the well-drilled productions by other companies which may seem to have greater pretensions, as well as larger resources.

Seasons at the Ballet Club, Hammersmith, and the New Theatre

The February season was followed by a longer one in April-May, during which Ashton's witty *Façade* was first given by the company, in its original version and with the original costumes which are retained by Ballet Rambert to the present day and are much preferred by many people to the revised choreography and décor, with their broader effects. With the help of Woizikovsky, Nijinsky's *L'Après-midi d'un Faune* was added to the repertoire. Karsavina, as well as Woizikovsky, was again associated with the company in a season at Hammersmith in June, during which she created the leading rôles in new ballets by Ashton and Salaman, and in a season at the New Theatre in September-October. Both the Russian dancers also accompanied them on their first appearance outside London when they visited Manchester for a week in October.

1931

New Choreographers and Designers

During the winter, performances continued at the Club on Sundays and on 12 November the programme included a new ballet by Ashton, *The Lady of Shalott*, with its striking simulation of a mirror, and Tudor's first essay in choreography, *Cross-garter'd*. In March, 1932, Tudor had a real success with *Lysistrata*, a ballet which long kept its place in the repertoire. In July came *The Garden*, Susan Salaman's diverting picture of the Fall, and *Unbowed*, a ballet by Sara Patrick which had music by Bax and, among other things, gave Hugh Stevenson his earliest opportunity for stage design and Hugh Laing his first rôle. Stevenson has since become one of the best and most prolific of English ballet designers and Hugh Laing rapidly proved himself a true romantic dancer, a verdict which has been endorsed in recent years by the public in America. *Unbowed* was the first ballet produced for the company by some one from outside. Although Mme Rambert produced six choreographers from her own " nursery," she has never hesitated to invite choreographers not associated with the company to compose ballets for her and in the record of the Repertoire the names of Ninette de Valois, Wendy Toye and several others will be found.

1931—1932

The winter brought two new ballets by Ashton, *Foyer de Danse* (October), in which he translated the world of Degas into action, and *Les Masques* (March), where the salted-almond flavour of Poulenc's music is matched by the witty choreography. In May, 1933, came Tudor's *Atalanta of the East*, an interesting and beautiful work, flawed only by indifferent Eastern music.

1932—1933

In the following October Andrée Howard ventured on choreography by making a new version of Susan Salaman's *Our Lady's Juggler* and in March composed *Mermaid* in association with her. *Mermaid* was remarkable for the imaginative results produced with the strictest economy of means, the whole story being vividly conveyed with only a dozen dancers and the slightest stage properties. Her work both as choreographer and designer will be considered later.

1933—1934

Summer Season of 1934

The Ballet Club Sundays were now supplemented by performances on a week-day evening and in the summer of 1934 there was a regular season at the Mercury, which opened with a new ballet, *Bar aux Folies-Bergère* by Ninette de Valois, inspired by Manet's famous picture, in which the world of Toulouse-Lautrec and the can-can was embodied in Markova's " La Goulue." In June came Ashton's *Mephisto Valse*, a masterpiece of concentrated force and expressiveness, in which Kyra Nijinsky later gave her unforgettable interpretation of Marguerite. She was the first of a series of guest artists, to be followed by such well-known names as Margot Fonteyn, June Brae, Robert Helpmann, Agnes de Mille, Bentley Stone and Norman Thomson.

New Ballets and New Dancers

The autumn season of 1934 opened in October with Tudor's first major work, *The Planets*, which, beautiful as it is on a small stage, is even finer on a large one. In this ballet, again, Kyra Nijinsky's spiritual depth was a direct inspiration for the role of The Mortal under Neptune. At the same time there was added to the repertoire *Alcina*, a suite of dances arranged by Andrée Howard for an entertainment called " Vauxhall Gardens," in which singing and ballet were combined. She followed this in January, 1935, with her *Cinderella*, in which the expert use of limited resources produces the illusion of a large scale production. In February there was a season at the Duke of York's Theatre during which Ashton produced *Valentine's Eve*. The spring brought Tudor's *Descent of Hebe*, the summer Susan Salaman's last ballet, *Circus Wings*.

1934—1935

After 1934 Markova was unable to continue her association with the Club and Pearl Argyle, Ashton and Turner made only rare appearances, but, in addition to the dancers already named, Peggy van Praagh was coming into prominence, and Frank Staff began to take leading rôles. Peggy van Praagh created a number in her own right and proved to be one of those invaluable dancers who can take over almost any type of part with success. She is a dancer of remarkable technique who joins great intensity of feeling to real gifts of comedy. Of Frank Staff it may be said that he showed the utmost promise from the start and that, great as has been his success in every type of rôle, he may yet reach further heights if his interest in choreography does not cause him to neglect his dancing.

In November, 1935, Andrée Howard produced her witty choreographic translation of Pope's *Rape of the Lock* and in the following January Tudor's Maupassant-like masterpiece, *Jardin aux Lilas*, had its première. In the summer of 1936 came the first visit by the company to the Birmingham Repertory Theatre, repeated in nearly every succeeding year. The autumn of 1936 brought *La Muse s'amuse*, Andrée Howard's delectable satire on the typical virtuoso and the typical hostess. In the following spring there was a season at the Duchess Theatre, with two new works, both of outstanding merit, and both deeply moving in their effect—Andrée Howard's *Death and the Maiden* and Tudor's *Dark Elegies*.

1935—1937

The Younger Generation

In the summer of 1937 Ballet Rambert made a tour of French watering places. In the autumn by visiting the Festival Theatre in Cambridge, they began their happy association with that town which has continued, at the Arts Theatre, until to-day.

Maude Lloyd, the leading *danseuse* from 1936 to 1940, was temporarily absent in the winter of 1937-1938 and the chief rôles were undertaken by Wendy Toye (who produced a new version of *Cross-Garter'd*), Prudence Hyman, Pamela Foster and June Brae. Another generation of young dancers was now coming to the fore, among them Deborah Dering, Celia Franca, Sally Gilmour, Charles Boyd and Leo Kersley. Deborah Dering, a dancer of great beauty and promise, left ballet before that promise was fulfilled. Charles Boyd, after taking a number of leading rôles and having a real success in his creation of "Mr. Tebrick", returned, on the outbreak of the war, to his native Australia. 1937—1938 Celia Franca's exotic beauty, her astonishing *ballon*, and poetic grace of movement, and Leo Kersley's strength and speed were for several years a rich asset to the company. Of the five, only Sally Gilmour has remained continually with Ballet Rambert, in which she has risen to the position of leading *danseuse*. Always promising, she attained fame in a night by her creation of the difficult leading rôle in *Lady into Fox*, an astonishing achievement for so young a dancer. Now that she has perfected her technique and revealed the rich depths of her nature, there are few if any dancers in this country to surpass her in both comedy and romantic ballet.

The First Ballets of Frank Staff and Walter Gore

In 1938 Frank Staff made his earliest attempt at choreography with *The Tartans*, a very perfect work in miniature, and a new version of *La Péri*, which was striking for the complete freshness of the choreographer's language. Walter Gore's originality was evident from the beginning. In the summer of 1938 he produced his first ballet, *Valse Finale*, with its atmosphere of affecting but tender sadness. It was later revised as *Les Valses*, a divertissement without story, to which some still prefer the earlier version. 1938—1939 He followed it in the spring of 1939 with *Paris-Soir*, an almost too complicated and *outré* picture of contemporary French life. In the summer there was a long season at the Mercury, notable for the production of Andrée Howard's dramatically poignant ballet, *Lady into Fox*, her first mature masterpiece. In December another season at the Duchess Theatre included the première of Staff's *Czernyana*, which combines witty satire of many types of ballet with some brilliantly inventive dancing.

Ballet at the Arts Theatre Club

Early in 1940 Ballet Rambert became associated with the Arts Theatre Club and for twenty months continued to give London seasons there, besides considerably extending the range of its provincial activities. The first season at the Arts Theatre opened on 8 February with a new ballet by Walter Gore, *Cap over Mill*, which had some happy touches, though neither the music nor the theme seemed quite congenial to him. In 1940 May, during a visit to Cambridge, came the production of Staff's *Peter and the Wolf*, which had an outstanding success, alike for the cleverness of the choreography, the excellence of the dancing and the brilliant décor by Guy Sheppard.

In June, 1940, Ballet Rambert was united with The London Ballet, which had for some time been one of the companies performing at the Arts Theatre Club.

NOTE ON THE LONDON BALLET, 1938-1941

When Tudor left the Mercury in the summer of 1937 to form his own company, he began by giving a week of performances jointly with Agnes de Mille at the Oxford Playhouse (14-19 June) under the name of Dance Theatre. It was then that his *Gallant Assembly* was first produced. But it was not until December, 1938, that Tudor's company (now called The London Ballet) began to give regular performances at Toynbee Hall with a repertoire consisting of some of the ballets which he had produced at the Mercury, together with *Judgment of Paris*, *Soirée Musicale* and *Gala Performance* and the enlargement of *The Planets* by the addition of "Mercury". For dancers he had not only Maude Lloyd, Peggy van Praagh and Hugh Laing, who had created leading rôles in his ballets while he was with the Ballet Rambert, but also a number of other dancers of outstanding ability or promise, among whom may be mentioned Gerd Larsen, Charlotte Bidmead, Pauline Clayden, Sylvia Hayden, Guy Massey and David Paltenghi. By the end of April, 1939, eleven performances had been given.

The war brought an end to these activities, and Tudor and Laing accepted invitations, which had been given to them in the previous summer, to work in the United States with Ballet Theatre. The London Ballet remained in being under the direction of Maude Lloyd and Peggy van Praagh, and on 30 November, 1939, became the first company to take part in the scheme for turning the Arts Theatre Club into a home for ballet in London. *Pas des Déesses* (Lester) was produced on the opening night and four more ballets were added in the next six months, including *The Seasons* (Staff) and, above all, Andrée Howard's beautiful and evocative *Fête Étrange*. In June, 1940, the increasing call-up of male dancers made it advisable for London Ballet to join forces with Ballet Rambert, to which several items in the repertoire were common, and the two companies continued together as Rambert-London Ballet until September, 1941.

More New Dancers

Something should now be said about the chief dancers who came to the company from London Ballet. Gerd Larsen and Charlotte Bidmead had taken leading rôles in Tudor's ballets in the Toynbee Hall days and continued to do good work with the combined companies. Pauline Clayden and David Paltenghi advanced rapidly with the greater opportunities which the fuller repertoire afforded, and have done work of increasing importance since, with the Sadler's Wells Ballet. Sylvia Hayden remained with Ballet Rambert longer. She had a particular success in *Enigma Variations* and in several rôles which had been associated with Maude Lloyd. It is to be hoped that her present transference to the field of drama is only temporary. Here, too, may be mentioned David Martin, who came to Ballet Rambert from Igor Schwezoff at the end of 1939 and gradually established his position in the company. He gave excellent performances of "The Faun" in *L'Après-midi d'un Faune* and "Pierrot" in *Carnaval* and his rapidly developing technique and innate capacity for losing himself in the characters he portrayed made it likely that he would be a leading member of the company after the war. His death in a flying accident in November, 1943, a few months after he had gained his wings in the Glider Pilot Regiment, was a real loss to English ballet.

The " Blitz " Surmounted

The Blitz which assailed London in September, 1940, threatened to end all theatrical activity, but actually had the result of making ballet more popular than ever. " Lunch Ballet " (from 1 o'clock to 2 o'clock), which began on 16 September, was so successful that soon three performances of one hour's duration were given each day. For twelve months the company continued to perform in London and the provinces and during this period several new ballets were produced. *Enigma Variations* (November, 1940) showed that Frank Staff could compose successfully in the symphonic manner as well as he had mocked at its absurdities, and *Czerny 2* (May, 1941) was as finely inventive and satirical as *Czernyana*, a dance of " Ébats avec corde " being specially delightful. During the summer Walter Gore composed several dances for himself and Sally Gilmour which were commissioned by and first performed at the Oxford Ballet Club and later added to the repertoire of the company. *Bartlemas Dances* revealed again the gaiety and tenderness which had been apparent in parts of *Paris-Soir*, while *Confessional* had the novelty of using the recitation of Browning's poem as well as some music of Sibelius for its accompaniment and gave Sally Gilmour a deeply emotional rôle.

1940—1941

The Ballet in Eclipse

In September, 1941, the proprietor of the Arts Theatre Club decided to discontinue his ballet activities and Mme Rambert found herself prevented by legal difficulties from maintaining her company independently. Some of the dancers joined other companies, some were called up for the services, but others accepted temporary engagements and continued to practise at the Mercury.

Ballet Rambert Resurrecta

At last, in March, 1943, the obstacles were overcome, the dancers were brought together and the Ballet Rambert rose again, phoenix-like, and began, under the auspices of C.E.M.A., a series of tours of munition factories, service camps and provincial towns, preceded by a memorable evening performance in their old home at the Mercury Theatre, when *Carnival of Animals*, a new light ballet by Andrée Howard, had its first performance.

In spite of all difficulties, this newly-reconstituted company had maintained its artistic standards and ideals, for Marie Rambert has always had the gift of making good her losses and imbuing the newcomers with the spirit of their predecessors. In Sally Gilmour the company had a leading dancer of rare quality and if the chief *danseur*, Robert Harrold, had little previous experience, he made up for any technical deficiency by the sympathy and poetry of his performance.

1943—1944

London saw the company for one week only in 1943, at Brockwell Park, but in 1944 there was a spring season at the Mercury, followed by a longer summer season at Hammersmith. Joan McClelland, who had done good work in minor parts for several years, now showed in leading rôles great emotional strength and intensity and a remarkable poise and beauty of line and Sara Luzita, another dancer of rare loveliness, began to come into prominence. Best of all, Walter Gore and Frank Staff, both choreographers as well as dancers, had been restored to the company after a period of service with the armed forces.

During the subsequent autumn tour two new ballets of exceptional quality were produced. In *The Fugitive* Andrée Howard has combined the haunting quality of *Fête Étrange* with the dramatic force of *Lady into Fox* and achieved a masterpiece, while Walter Gore has matched the wit and liveliness of Britten's *Simple Symphony* with choreography which is as beautiful as it is gay.

1944—1945 A single week at Hammersmith in the summer of 1945 gave London its first sight of the two new ballets and brought into clearer notice the merit of some of the younger dancers, among whom may be named Joyce Graeme, Brenda Hamlyn, Margaret Scott and Jean Stokes. During the annual visit to Birmingham the production of the second act of *Giselle* showed, once again, the virtues of Mme Rambert's revivals of the classics, and revealed Sally Gilmour as an ideal exponent of the title-rôle. The autumn brought the company to Hammersmith for another week, when a new ballet by Frank Staff, *Un Songe*, with its beautiful tender movements, was first seen in London and another promising youngster, Annette Chappell had her debut.

A continental tour, under E.N.S.A., was due to begin after Christmas and, in the meantime, the first act of *Giselle* and a new work by Walter Gore were in active preparation for production on their return. Ballet Rambert does not rest on its laurels and its future holds the promise of being as exciting and as successful as its past.

Sixteen Years of Ballet Rambert

When the year ended the company could look back on sixteen years of outstanding artistic achievement and face the future with undiminished hope and confidence. Ballet Rambert provided dancers, choreographers and ballets for the pioneer efforts of the Camargo Society in 1930-33, its members have given added strength to many other companies, and its own repertoire is extensive and important, its dancers assured in technique and expression. If only the difficulty of securing a theatre could be overcome and regular seasons be given in the West End of London, the new public which has grown up in the past few years would join its many provincial admirers in appreciating what ballet connoisseurs have long known—that Ballet Rambert is one of the major forces in the modern art of the dance.

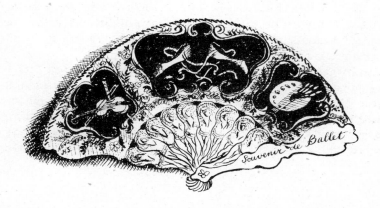

THE CHOREOGRAPHERS AND THEIR BALLETS

IT MAY BE AS WELL to say something first on the general question whether it is true that the ballets in the repertoire are in the main of a special type to which the term " chamber ballet " has been applied. Certainly the small stage of the Mercury, which cannot accommodate more than about sixteen dancers, and the direct contact with the audience have had some effect both on the choreographers and the dancers. But the analogy from music is probably a false one. The art of Pavlova was no less manifest when she performed Fokine's *Le Cygne* in a large theatre and no one has suggested that ballets with only a few dancers such as *Le Spectre de la Rose* and *L'Après-midi d'un Faune* should be confined to small stages. The *danseuse* who can create an illusion by personality and by imaginative and expressive movement when the audience is only a few yards away will be even more successful when she has the aid of distance, and a dancer who has trained himself to appear to move freely in a confined space will, in fact, move more freely when he has room in which to let himself go.

So, too, with the choreographer. It is clear that the small stage precludes the use of large-scale mass movements, and that the nearness of the audience makes faking impossible and encourages subtlety of effect. But this limitation of resources forces the choreographer to use them to the utmost and most of the ballets have positively gained from the transfer to a larger stage. Nor must it be forgotten that a number of the ballets in the repertoire were, in fact, originally produced on stages of normal size and that some of them cannot be put on to the stage of the Mercury. It is interesting, also, to observe what good use has been made, by both choreographers and designers, of the permanent staircase at the back of the Mercury stage (e.g., in *Le Boxing, Foyer de Danse, Les Masques, Cinderella*, etc.).

Frederick Ashton

Frederick Ashton was the first of the choreographers in point of date and the earliest of them to gain fame outside. After his first tentative beginnings in *A Tragedy of Fashion* (1926), he spent a year in the Ida Rubinstein Ballet, working with Massine and Nijinska, from both of whom he learnt much, especially from the latter. He soon showed a capacity to invent new and beautiful movements and has always known how to make the most of the individual qualities of the dancers he employs. Even in the earlier ballets which have fallen into disuse there was evidence of his ability to use the groupings and movements of the *corps de ballet* to enhance and set off the principal characters, a good example being his treatment of the " Companions " in *La Péri* (1931). Two of his earlier ballets remain as fresh and captivating as when they were first produced. *Capriol Suite* (1930) is still an ideal divertissement, inventive and varied, producing its effects by dancing rather than by characterization. *Façade* (1931), especially in its original form, is a typical piece of English humour, avoiding vulgarity and burlesque, and successfully matching the composer's mockery of different types of music. *Foyer de Danse* (1932) needs a " Maître de ballet " who is a good actor as well as an efficient dancer, and allows the " Étoile " to display her technique as well as to parody the vanity and foibles of the temperamental *ballerina*. It has not been equalled by any of the other attempts to translate the pictorial world of Degas into movement.

Les Masques (1933) has a sharp quality which perfectly suits the piquant music. It is a witty commentary on the cross-purposes of lovers at a Society Ball and the stylized choreography keeps it on a plane of sophistication. *Mephisto Valse* (1934), short as it is, has all the emotional effect of a full length romantic ballet. The first raptures of Marguerite's love and her final anguish give great opportunities to the dancer's powers of dramatic expressiveness. In both these ballets, the five or six dancers who make up, as it were, a miniature *corps de ballet*, are particularly well used, in the one case to point the effect by their mannered movements, and in the other to charge the atmosphere with the intensity of their dancing. In *Valentine's Eve* (1935) Ashton matched the mood of Ravel's various " Valses " by the qualities of his characters : the nobility of the poet, the coquettishness of the girl to whom he gives his heart, and so on. It was a ballet with an atmosphere of its own. *Passionate Pavane* (1936) is, so far, the latest work produced by Ashton for Ballet Rambert. It is a revised version of a Pas de Trois composed for Lopokova, Turner and the choreographer in 1930 and its stately formal movements accord perfectly with Dowland's music and the beautiful rich costumes.

There is a lyrical quality in nearly all of Ashton's ballets, and in each the characters are developed and the story told in terms of pure dancing.

Susan Salaman

Susan Salaman had a lesser talent, but, within its limits, her ballets were always theatrically effective. Her best work was in the *Sporting Sketches* (1930-31), with their humorous caricatures of the English worship of athletics. The dance movements she employs are not in themselves unusual, but are so used as to seem particularly fresh and witty. These miniature ballets need no more than half-a-dozen dancers, but in other works Miss Salaman showed an ability to use ampler forces to advantage and it is a matter for regret that her full development as a choreographer was cut short by illness.

Antony Tudor

Antony Tudor's first ballet, *Cross-Garter'd* (1931), was an adaptation of the Garden Scene from " Twelfth Night." If it was more successful in detail than as a whole, he showed from the outset great originality of conception and novelty of choreographic

OUR LADY'S JUGGLER *(Salaman, 1930)*

Marie Rambert and Harold Turner, with four acolytes

4   W. Chappell and W. Gore
in FACADE *(Ashton, 1931)*

Diana Gould, with F. Ashton and W. Chappell

CAPRIOL SUITE *(Ashton, 1930)*

3

Elisabeth Schooling,
F. Staff,
W. Gore,
and Andrée Howard
in 1934

5 A TRAGEDY OF FASHION
(Ashton, 1926)

Marie Rambert and F. Ashton
with E. Vincent and F. James

LE BOXING *(Salaman, 1931)* 6

Maude Lloyd, W. Chappell,
Diana Gould, R. Doone
and A. Tudor

CROSS-GARTER'D *(Tudor, 1931)*

7 E. Schooling, Maude Lloyd, B. Cuff, R. Gamble, P. Hyman, W. Gore, A. Tudor, W. Chappell.

Pearl Argyle
in
LE SPECTRE DE LA ROSE
(Fokine)

8

Prudence Hyman and
W. Gore in 1931

CARNAVAL *(Fokine)*

10 D. Martin in 1941

32   H. Laing, Peggy van Praagh, A. Tudor and Maude Lloyd

JARDIN AUX LILAS *(Tudor, 1936)*

33   Revival 1944: Sally Gilmour, F. Staff and Joan McClelland

THE RAPE OF THE LOCK
(Howard, 1935)

The toilet of Belinda

34

Andrée Howard and Pearl Argyle, with S. Morfield, A. Gee, O. Sarel and B. Ke

CINDERELLA *(Howard, 1935)*

35

S. Morfield, F. Ashton, Pearl Argyle, W. Gore and M. Lloyd

LA MUSE S'AMUSE
(Howard, 1936)

Andrée Howard and F. Staff *(centre)*, with W. Toye, A. Gee, S. Gilmour,
C. Franca, D. Dering and E. Schooling in 1937

37

PASSIONATE PAVANE
(Ashton, 1936)

F. Staff, Maude Lloyd
and W. Gore

Andrewes, S. Gilmour, L. Kersley, D. Dering, C. Franca, W. Gore, W. Toye, F. Staff

CROSS-GARTER'D
(Toye, 1937)

THE DESCENT OF HEBE
(Tudor, 1935)

39   Elisabeth Schooling and A. Tudor   40   A. Tudor

41   Elisabeth Schooling, A. Tudor, H. Laing and Maude Lloyd

F. Staff,
D. Paltenghi,
and Maude Lloyd

LA FÊTE ÉTRANGE
(*Howard*, 1940)

57

The same with H. Legerton, T. Langfield, P. Clayden and M. Boam (*down the stairs*), S. Hayden, D. Dering, C. Bidmead, E. Hamilton, S. Reeves (*at back*), and A. Kelly and E. Schooling (*right*)

Celia Franca,
W. Gore, Lulu Dukes
and L. Kersley

PETER AND
THE WOLF
(*Staff*, 1940)

59

60   Joan McClelland, J. Wade, S. Morfield, D. Martin

61   Sally Gilmour

Elisabeth Schooling, Sally Gilmour, M. Bayston and W. Gore

SIMPLE SYMPHONY (*Gore*, 1944)

Sally Gilmour and Elisabeth Schooling, with W. Gore, S. Newby, M. Bayston, M. Holmes and Paula Hinton

72   GISELLE, Act II (*Coralli and Perrot*) in 1945:   W. Gore, Sally Gilmour and Joyce Graeme

THE FUGITIVE (*Howard, 1944*)

73   Sally Gilmour, Joan McClelland and W. Gore, with Brenda Hamlyn, M. Bayston, M. Holmes and Marjorie Field

COMPLETE REPERTOIRE

(Revised to 30 November, 1945)

NOTE

Titles of ballets performed since 1943 are marked *. Performances at the Headquarters of Ballet Rambert at Ladbroke Road are described as Mercury Theatre, though that name did not come into use until the autumn of 1933. Dancers' names are given in the form in use to-day. In the lists following each ballet the name of the creator of a rôle is marked *, followed in round brackets by the names of the chief dancers who have since taken it. As a rule only the principal rôles are given, or the principal dances in a divertissement. When a ballet was produced elsewhere first and the creator of a rôle did not subsequently dance it for Ballet Rambert the name is enclosed in square brackets (e.g. Lopokova in Façade). Tudor's Adam and Eve and Gallant Assembly, Wendy Toye's Leçon Apprise and Ashton's Lord of Burleigh, which have not been performed by Ballet Rambert in the normal repertoire, are included for the sake of completeness.

[ADAM AND EVE
Choreography : A. Tudor. Music : Lambert. Décor : John Banting. First produced (for Camargo Society), 4 Dec., 1932, at Adelphi Th. *Not performed by Ballet Rambert.*
Adam, *A. Dolin ; *Eve,* *Prudence Hyman ; *Serpent,* *A. Tudor].

ALCINA SUITE
Choreography : Andrée Howard. Music : Handel (*Entrance,* Purcell). Décor : A. Howard. First produced (in " Vauxhall Gardens "), as La Belle Assemblée, 11 Oct., 1934, at Mercury Th., and by Ballet Rambert, 28 Oct., 1934, at Mercury Th.
Alcina, *Maude Lloyd (Elisabeth Schooling, Wendy Toye) ; *Her Lovers,* *A. Tudor. *H. Laing (F. Staff, W. Gore) ; *Tambourine,* *Elisabeth Schooling (Maria Sanina, Ann Gee).

*APRÈS-MIDI D'UN FAUNE, L'
Choreography : V. Nijinsky. Music : Debussy. Costumes : Bakst. First produced by Diaghilev Ballet, 29 May, 1912, at Th. du Châtelet, Paris, revived for Ballet Rambert (by Woizikovsky), 20 April, 1931, at Mercury Th.
The Faun, W. Chappell (H. Laing, F. Staff, L. Kersley, D. Martin) ; *Nymph,* Diana Gould (Pearl Argyle, Maude Lloyd, Daphne Gow, Celia Franca, Sally Gilmour, Sara Luzita).

ATALANTA OF THE EAST
Choreography : A. Tudor. Music : Szántó and Seelig (arr. of Eastern music). Décor : W. Chappell. First produced, 7 May, 1933, at Mercury Th.
Sita, *Pearl Argyle ; *Vikram,* *H. Laing ; *Goddess,* *Diana Gould (Anna Brunton) ; *King,* *A. Tudor.

AURORA'S WEDDING, DANCES FROM
Choreography : M. Petipa. Music : Tchaikovsky. Costumes : Andrée Howard. The complete ballet of " The Sleeping Beauty " was first produced, 15 Jan., 1890, at Maryinsky Th., St. Petersburg, revived (for Diaghilev Ballet) by Nijinska, 2 Nov., 1921, at Alhambra Th. The selection named " Aurora's Wedding " was first given in 1922, revived by Ballet Rambert, 16 Feb., 1931, at Mercury Th. Excerpts had been given previously.
Blue Bird pas de deux, Prudence Hyman (Alicia Markova, Helena Wolska, Nina Golovina, Deborah Dering, Celia Franca, Pauline Clayden) *and* H. Turner (L Woizikovsky, T. Slavinsky, R. Doone, W. Gore, F. Staff, L. Kersley) ; *Aurora,* Alicia Markova (Pearl Argyle, Maude Lloyd, Nina Golovina, Helena Wolska, Sylvia Hayden; Gerd Larsen).

*BAR AUX FOLIES-BERGÈRE
Choreography : Ninette de Valois. Music : Chabrier. Décor : W. Chappell. First produced, 15 May, 1934, at Mercury Th.
La Goulue, *Alicia Markova (Mona Inglesby, Andrée Howard, Maude Lloyd, Prudence Hyman, Celia Franca, Sally Gilmour, Nina Golovina, Gerd Larsen, Sara Luzita) ; *La fille au bar,* Pearl Argyle (Elisabeth Schooling, Sally Gilmour, Lisa Serova, Joan McClelland, Margaret Scott) ; *Grille d'Égout,* *Diana Gould (Doris Sonne, Tamara Svetlova, Pamela Foster, Celia Franca, etc.) ; *Valentin, garçon,* *F. Ashton (W. Gore, F. Staff, R. Harrold) ; *Le vieux Marcheur,* *Oliver Reynolds (W. Gore, A. Tudor, H. Laing, D. Macey, F. Staff, R. Doone, J. Andrewes, D. Martin, D. Paltenghi, M. Holmes).

*BARTLEMAS DANCES (BARTLEMAS FAIR)
Choreography : W. Gore. Music : Holst. Costumes : W. Chappell. First produced (for Oxford Ballet Club), 9 May, 1941 ; by Ballet Rambert, 13 May, 1941, at Arts Th., London.
Dancers, *Sally Gilmour *and* *W. Gore.

BOXING, LE
Choreography : Susan Salaman. Music : Berners. Décor : W. Chappell. First produced, 16 Feb., 1931, at Mercury Th.
The Sport Girl, *Maude Lloyd (Maria Sanina, Celia Franca, etc.) ; *The Trainer,* *A. Tudor (L. Kersley, J. Andrewes, D. Martin, etc.) ; *The Vamp de Luxe,* *Diana Gould (Maude Lloyd, Prudence Hyman, Wendy Toye, Pamela Foster, Lisa Serova) ; *The English Champion,* *R. Doone (W. Gore) ; *The American Champion,* *W. Chappell (F. Staff, J. Byron, L. Kersley).

CAP OVER MILL

Choreography: W. Gore. Music: Bate. Décor: Nadia Benois. First produced, 8 Feb., 1940, at Arts Th., London.
Vivandière, *Lisa Serova (Peggy van Praagh); *Army Surgeon*, *W. Gore; *Colonel*, *D. Martin; *Grand-daughter*, *Sally Gilmour (Susette Morfield).

*CAPRIOL SUITE

Choreography: F. Ashton. Music: Warlock. Décor: W. Chappell. First produced, 25 Feb., 1930, at Lyric Th., Hammersmith.
Tordion, *Andrée Howard (Susette Morfield, etc.) *and* *H. Turner (W. Gore, etc.); *Pavane*, *Diana Gould (Pearl Argyle, Maude Lloyd, Daphne Gow, Wendy Toye, Peggy van Praagh, etc.) *and* *F. Ashton, *W. Chappell (H. Turner, A. Tudor, H. Laing, etc.).

*CARNAVAL

Choreography: M. Fokine. Music: Schumann. Costumes: L. Bakst. First produced by Diaghilev Ballet, 4 June, 1910, at Opera, Paris; revived by Ballet Rambert, 20 Dec., 1930, at Lyric Th., Hammersmith.
Columbine, *Tamara Karsavina (Prudence Hyman, Alicia Markova, Tatiana Semenova, Sally Gilmour); *Chiarina*, Diana Gould (Pearl Argyle, Maude Lloyd, Sara Luzita, Sylvia Hayden, Joan McClelland, Joyce Graeme); *Papillon*, Andrée Howard (Prudence Hyman, Alicia Markova, Mona Inglesby, Elisabeth Schooling, Brenda Hamlyn, Annette Chappell); *Harlequin*, L. Woizikovsky (H. Turner, R. Doone, W. Gore, F. Staff, J. Moore); *Pierrot*, R. Stuart (A. Tudor, D. Martin, M. Holmes, J. Moore); *Eusebius*, F. Ashton (D. Paltenghi, R. Reid); *Pantalon*, W. Gore (W. Chappell, F. Staff, S. Newby).

*CARNIVAL OF ANIMALS

Choreography: Andrée Howard. Music: Saint-Saëns. Décor: A. Howard. First produced, before an invited audience, 26 Mar., 1943, at Mercury Th.
The Little Girl, *Elisabeth Schooling (Sally Gilmour); *The Lion*, *Iris Loraine (Pamela Sabine); *The Hen*, *Margaret Scott; *The Bantam*, *Olivia Sarel (Joan McClelland); *Tortoises*, *Nina Shelley *and* *M. Holmes; *The Kangaroo*, *Marguerite Stewart; *Aquarium*, *Sylvia Hayden, *Anne Ashley (Brenda Hamlyn); *Personage with long ears*, *R. Harrold (S. Newby); *Cuckoo*, *Sara Luzita (Elisabeth Schooling); *Girl with Birds*, *Sally Gilmour (Jean Stokes).

CINDERELLA

Choreography: Andrée Howard. Music: Weber. Décor: A. Howard. First produced, 6 Jan., 1935, at Mercury Th.
Cinderella, *Pearl Argyle (Maude Lloyd, Deborah Dering, Nina Golovina); *The Prince*, *F. Ashton (H. Laing, F. Staff, J. Byron); *The Ugly Sisters*, *Elisabeth Schooling, *Andrée Howard (Ann Gee); *Fairy Godmother*, *Susette Morfield; *Court Hairdresser*, *W. Gore, F. Staff, L. Kersley; *A Courtier*, *W. Gore (F. Staff, J. Byron, L. Kersley, A. Rassine); *First Guest*, *Maude Lloyd (Maria Sanina, Peggy van Praagh, Celia Franca, Anna Lendrum).

CIRCUS WINGS

Choreography: Susan Salaman. Music: Milhaud. Décor: S. Salaman. First produced, 16 June, 1935, at Mercury Th.
Queen of the Circus, *Maude Lloyd; *Ringmaster*, *A. Tudor; *Boxing Kangaroo*, *F. Staff; *His Trainer*, *W. Gore; *Trapezists*, *Elisabeth Schooling, *F. Staff, *L. Edwards; *The Tattooed Lady*, *Peggy van Praagh; *Performing Pony*, *Susette Morfield; *Seal*, *Tamara Svetlova (Isobel Reynolds).

*CONFESSIONAL

Choreography: W. Gore. To the poem by Browning and music by Sibelius. Costumes: Andrée Howard. First produced (for Oxford Ballet Club), 9 May, 1941; by Ballet Rambert, 21 Aug., 1941, at Arts Th., London.
Dancers, *Sally Gilmour *and* *W. Gore; *Speaker*, M. Dobson (D. Martin, Eunice Rogers).

*CRICKET, LE

Choreography: Susan Salaman. Music: Benjamin. Décor: S. Salaman. First produced, 20 Dec., 1930, at Lyric Th., Hammersmith.
Bowler, *A. Tudor, (W. Gore, L. Kersley, etc.); *Batsman*, *W. Chappell (W. Gore, F. Staff, J. Byron, etc.); *Umpire*, *R. Stuart (W. Gore, F. Staff, J. Andrewes, D. Martin, etc.).

CROQUIS DE MERCURE

Choreography: Andrée Howard. Music: Satie. Costumes: A. Howard. First produced, 13 Feb., 1938, at Mercury Th.
Mercury, *W. Gore (F. Staff, L. Kersley); *Danse de Tendresse*, *Andrée Howard (Celia Franca, Maude Lloyd, Sally Gilmour) *and* *F. Staff (W. Gore, L. Kersley).

CROSS-GARTER'D (Two Versions)

Music: Frescobaldi. Setting: Pamela Bocquet. Costumes *after* Burnacini.
1, Choreography: A. Tudor. First produced, 12 Nov., 1931, at Mercury Th.
Olivia, *Maude Lloyd (Diana Gould); *Maria*, *Prudence Hyman; *Malvolio*, *A. Tudor (R. Gamble); *Sir Toby*, *W. Gore; *Sir Andrew*, *R. Gamble (A. Tudor).
2, Choreography: Wendy Toye. First produced, 14 Nov., 1937, at Mercury Th.
Olivia, *Wendy Toye (Maude Lloyd).